Poetry of weeping willows

Sofia Hällgren

Cyberwit.net
HIG 45 Kaushambi Kunj, Kalindipuram
Allahabad - 211011 (U.P.) India
http://www.cyberwit.net
Tel: +(91) 9415091004
E-mail: info@cyberwit.net

Printed at Repro India Limited.

Contents

1. The like.

The Madonna in the ,
Made of glass.
Kiss its feet, Oh anguished saint.
Footsteps on the pews, angelic
Footsteps.
I kiss its feet. The stained glass wings
Of the transparent butterfly flies
In the air.
Inhale and believe.
People sit in the Pews
Nodding like flowers underneath
The sea.
Holiness.

2. Birth.

For years I have slaved
I want to kiss you
You're Angelus.
After Angelus.
I watch a painting
Of Kafka.
Your sperm in a jar.
Youre the one.
Ghosts Of neurosedyne children.
I am a death.
I look to you.
Smiling
 Youre the like.
Vampire still haunting me
Outside my window

3. Stoneangel

Come bless
Me
Hands grasping
Mine.
Edith whartons poetry
Read out loud to dead children
You the one.
Ghosttown
His.
Boy , face like a pharoah.
 Memories black&white.
Past gunfights .
Billy
The kid.
Body of a ghost.

4. Origami

She lies in a hospitalbed,
Birdlike, she lies there.
Around her seagulls and stars.
Silver meets gold as doors open and shut
Tight around her.
She lies there,
Ghostlike.
The seagulls fly confused in the air
Around her.
She smiles faerylike and watches them.

Moonlight later,
Silver, like a paper Moon
On the walls of the hospital.
She makes origami stars
And mobile birds.

5. Elsindor.

Shes got a tattoo of a swirl
And Brown long curly hair.
And bracelets of turquoise
And rings of Dolphins.
Shes awake and sweet lullabies
Are played for her,
The selkie and the sealwoman
Are played for her by the inuits.
She walks the beach and inside of her
Is a sacred Temple of the occult.

And Inside if her is a sacred Temple of   the dragon rouge.
A Golden occult symbol and some
Lilac galaxies and some planets of such
Beauty none can Imagine.
Buddha smiles Inside yellow astral
Galaxy Inside nirvana rain.
She is a portal within the paranormal Gates
And the mother of all things paranormal
She is a stargate amd has the key to Elsindor.

6. nothing.

Stars and space, a room lit up
And a table. And on it, a fashion magazine. Shes sitting there
Reading, not knowing what to do next.
She astral jumps and ends up in a parallell world. She meets
people there,
People living their lives, loving their gods. She enters her reality
again,
And reads about trees in space
And studies quantum physics
On the miscatonic university.
Shes got a computer that talks
To parallel Worlds.
And chats to a japanese woman
Every day who wears a red and White bikerjacket.
But in that other world Shes got no
Idea that girl exists.
Her sister is a dog there.
She borrows books about
Saturn and Pluto
And then she reads

Peter Pan and wendy.
And the lost boys.

She watched a dvd on how to do I ching
And how to read fortunes.
And visits a haunted house and reads about occult stuff.
Its big red house with two storeys
And the found books from the turn of the century occult.

Images sewn Into the quilt, of me and women, medieval.
She marries her husband who is an
Insect in that other world.
And in there, there are beings
And in there there are green Hills
And meadows and houses and they read and watch tv
She hangs up small Skulls and

Stones from strings and a plastic unicorn

 And a plastic unicorn.

And seashell.

She reads about dimension
And
Monsters and seamonsters.

About Chutulhu
Then she sees the artwork
Come to life. To tell her
Shes the mother of all things
Paranormal.

7.

The weirdos are here.

She is in space.
Amongst stars and crying of Dead people.
The spaceship flies in space
Past balloons and spaceship and planets.
Abandonded and alone is the man
In the spaceship.
She tell him , the girl with
The Bunny ears, that shes there for hum
But he forgets when he enters heaven.
His arms are full of tattoos and
Her stommach is full with antichrist
Baby now.
His legs are in pants now, yellow
With Black stripes.

9.

Inside of the space are monks,
Space is full of Gothgirls
Painting the sky with stars
Monks,stand in space.
Holding skulls.
The faeries fly around in it,
Having fun
A man with a cross in his
Forehead reads voodoo.
And a girl puts up stars
From the space
In strings of her mask
And a vampire poster.
She Burns and catches
A Star with her hands.
A faery is Inside of it.
A girl , she brings out the
Magician.
A girl swings in space pn a swing

10. sky.

I am Lacrimosa
Requiem
I a question
Willst the soul eye of Mozart
See the heaven?
I art thou neck.

.

 moist
Walls, while
Glowing flowers glow in hell.

11. Thou.

I am in the haunted house
Water Between the walls
A womans haunting voice.
She is there, time.
She walked there,
Crying along with the walks
Of time.
Paper people, silhouettes.
Walking like stickfigures.
They are in the mirror,
Waterpeople.
So she is.
A watch strikes

12. Waterfaces.

I am.
Artwork by a dark poet.
I love you, the entity whispers,
Through walls of time.
Ghost footsteps, rattle and hum.

Tea.
I am.
Beyond time and space
A wandering ghost.
Planets spin,
Like spun sugar.
Walking on Clouds.
Never coming back.
A constant high.
Its Good with tea.

13. I am

The like of ye.
I a Caterpillar, spun silk.
So Fair.
Tree of the moon, silver.
Tree of the sin, golden.
Her. Walking towards
Her house.
Fabric of the moon
On her. Watching herself in a pool.
Red hair, blue eyes.
I am. You who is.
I used to be a Free spiritu.
Sand drift away, space and
Time.
Door of heaven opened.
She walks inside .
Opened up her door and walks Into moon
And sun. Geishas.
I.

14. Murder

Of a bygone president.
_tears of mechanical
Dreams.
Dreams of a Princess
Lying on lit de parade
Holding a Pink french fairytale book.
In her hand, a dove.
Politics, origami boat she sailed on
Towards an unknown shore.
Made by papier mache.
A well Known pastime, a teardrenched hug.
Ghost of someone.
Death by the roadside.

15. I a thy.

I a question
A warm tear,
A faery
I answer
I question.
I.
The one.
Werewolf stake.
II
A weathermap
A day, a blanket worn by
An origami swallov.
I a Caterpillar
I a grassy hill.
Skeleton of a beetle buried on a Hill.
A dad who worried too much
And smokes a pipe
And who thinks about Hitler,
The ww2, the bombs and the camps.
Grandmas groovy box.
Mafias wives.
We think we're better than the Mafias wives.
Along comes unbirthday, monkeys party
And the wife of a druglord.

Cigars Rolled on the thighs
Of chinese Virgins,
In the darkest part of Chinatown,
Where few dare to tread.
Time Clouds, Peru.
California wine, new york
Models and retired ballerinas.
Lo and behold!
An idea.
Writer black&White
Sunglasses faded.
I was.
California hippie.
Flower power are we.
Bound to you.
Like ashes in the grievers hand
Outside the crematorium.
Summer.
Smoke sweet hasch, eat
Strawberries, yet die anyway.
Meadow, I loved him well.

16. I feel the same wind of San Francisco

Killing time with new yorker
Magazine
In my hands.
A "In cold blood" copy lies
On my chest. Scorned, rejected
And dislike, I packed my bags
And flew to California.
Well there, I checked Into a motel
And saw a aquarium

I felt like a angry boy.
I cut my hair, so like Rosemarys
Baby. I loved that movie.
I watched parents, watched old People,
Went to New York.
Slept with a rich badboy.
Left the very same det, took
Berries from a graveyard , where
The berries taste like no other berries.
I were the Only one alive.
Hurried to Woodstock and an artgallery.
Left for an old friend who was dying.
We talked while the sky bled
The sun slit its wrists to bleed
Across the sky.
I was left with the words live
!
I went back to the sky of Philadelphia,
Bleeding in the heart.

17. Moon

Moonchild, moonbeam.
Her names
She had two navels
And a pregnancy
Both were lies.
A conjunction
Of a magician.
She left for HP Lovecrafts
Miscatonic university.
A blink 82 song
Kept her awake.
I Will see the Palace
Of nothing, sun and moon.
I a wandering jew.
Planets.
Spinning
Faeries set ablaze
Fire.
Fire walk with me
Again.
Woods.
Sounds of Children,
All alone in a tent,
Blair witch.
Face no eyes

Hospital ghosts.
Open up the Gates.

18.

Channel twilight zon,
She puts her hands against
The screen-
Theyre heere.
I am lover of an insect man
In Another dimension
The boy gets corn in his hands, that
Appears and reappears by magic.
Tv showing static.
The girl is gone .
Black Magic, the witch lives in a apt,formelly owned by a
satanist
Now on deathrow.

19.

Falling
Like a doll
In a river, floating.
In the backseat of a car,
Put in.
I float ..
I cold one
I Blessed be.
She victim of s carcrash,.A Kennedy
Let her die.
She sits in a couch
On the other side.
Welcome
Into the circus.
Were all dead here.

20.

Nobody.
I a fly
On Another dimension,
My sister calls me from
The other side where the is a fish.
We are Cherry blossom
Sunset.
I a boat.
Fishermen dug a grave
For their adversary.
I a dark occult child.
Im stupid
Wormeaten.
Skeletal dance
Central for the funny
Smoking.

21

I a walked backwards.
I a nibwit. I a walking Star
Planets bow for me
I lucky outlaw.
Gunslinger and daughter of the
Hangman has nuffn on me.
Hangmands daughter.
I could kill half a dozen men
While youre screwing around.
I sit in the room On the other side
While you hold the remote control.
We are better than the wild bunch.
I am breathing.
Star of Betlehem
Trio of wise men.

22.

I an outlaw sister
Wild west
Devils child.
Whiskey running down my Throat

Of nothing 213

Dahmers room
Number
Haunted

Victorian furniture
Made by a graveyard grave digger.

23.

The girl swings in space
On a swing of stars.
Planets
Stirling.
The baby mouse eats.
Lsd cares.

24.

We
Eating an icecream
At a chinese restaurant.
Lanterns glow.
She walks to her car.
The kids look at her, as she approaches them.
She is smiling. Scents of
Opium. They ask if they can use her phone.
Her nod. They suddenly get Black eyes.
 Beks.
Black eyed kids, beks. Were demons, sent here to kill you.
They attack her.

25.

Run. Urn memories.
Her face stripper.
Moon pretty.
Loves somebody.
Har hand and Dominon.
Greek amphitheatre.
Stay gold.
En ergy.
Tao Chi.
The suns Temple. A Lion is on a table with astrologi al signs.
They water heaven with their tears.
Lilies. Scents of heaven.
Babylon.
They got urns of Clay.
The dripping rain of Africa.
Memory.
The zoo York

26.

The chinese woman with her funeral
Grooving her time in halfwitted Chapels. Her porcelaine doll
face.
Heart of Rainbow. Her dead talk to her
Rice falls from her.
Small Worlds are in the Rice.
27. Dead
Dead. Planets from mars
On the pavement.
Aeroplanes lift
Youre there in.
Inside the aeroplane are People from dreams.
Her haunted face.
Theyre disappearing Into Another world forever…
Back to the viewer.
Magenta

27. Weirdo.

We are spiritu. Ectoplasma on the floor.
A seance in the mall.
They are born Into nothing
St elmos fire
Stars in her eyes.

Youth
Your tears Shed over him.
Theyre with be.
Fallen in the fall of antibes
Isle of Children.
He. Spirits.
Dreams like memories

28.

Dead Caterpillar
Silk, so fair.
Indochine. Fairest fairy Dreams.
Theyre a beautiful Ghost
Heavens most Lovely.
Death couldnt be better.
I am allt of saint Elmo.
College secret society
Drinking with the witches.
Glowed with the fire Of youth

29.

Se are.
Leopard Will come to the meeting
Treasure of Bluebeard
They arent ghosts
Of Milky way.
We are Milky way of dust
Deathstars universe.

30.

Milk of cow
Romelus and Remus are feeding from.
Moon come up for tea?
Good and just
Pale and space on a swing of stars
The galaxy.
Of demons.
Tv shows static.
Memory nostalgi
Wings of butterfly. Har heart.
Grotesque fairy heart.

31.

I am inside of ye.
The rival.
The där, my ex.
The child, me.

32.

The tv Lion isnt.

33.

Me. I artwork in the party
Ive decorated is li a witch would.
Wherein are witches.
Victorian furniture.
Astral teacher taught about match
And wicca.
Moon move me.
Like a homeless boy.
Dying.
Astral.

35.

Your hand in it a heartshaped
Stone. I a wandering
Prayer. Stone.
Beach of magick.
The White,Stone.
Help from angels.
He a faery.
Zen.

36.

I see a picture of Kafka.
And a image of me as dead.
I.   Goblins yellow eyed
Witches trees in
The trench.
Rain falling a wizard.
See a seer of eons.
As I walked up to the wizard,
Her face lit up.

3 7.

A face of neon
I a dreamtree
In which you go to dream.
I sent there to dream

I was one of the few to go there.
The trees robots
Forever.
I look out.
I see a fantasy landscape
Of trees, wizard
And demons.
I see dreameaters and the spirits
That knit clothes.
Fabric half,so fair
Made by Fairy breath.

39

Wolfmoon
Were halfway there
Wolf bloodred moon
Means death.
I a Stone of a wizard
I a cry of the paleolithix
 they take my blessings.

40

Im a the like.
Stoneage neolithic
I am wanderer upon the moon

I am the girl who loved the Moon
I am deep astral theatre.
With shadows, they make theatre.
I the unloved.
Galaxy of the dead.
Isle of the dead,
We promise to return.
They gather among us,
The dead. Shrouds and
Ghost spectres.
I am.
Door of the isle of the dead.
Open.

41. The like

Ghost in Shrouds
I loved you.
Your shadow face.
Your name, you refuse me.
My love is unrequited.
Im not allowed to speak your name.
You never Said anything about a tattoo.
He he

42

Theyre.
A dead.
I a once wise woman
Now very dead.
You.
Ice woman.
Mirror upon the Wall
For drinking these dark victorian
Mirrors again.
I, the spellbound.
I once were faery.
Now naught
Stars are falling Into the river
Of Ophelia.
Ghostchildren song nonny,
Nonny, nonny with her.
Leaves fall to cover the maiden.
Pregnant by Hamlet.
She smiles, surviving night
And eternal death.
Flowers in her hair.

43

Damned
Its about a girl
Who is damned
Birth by a Bitch of Babylon
As her dad, Satani.
A pentacle reversed.
If .
What heaven knows.
She cried
To the mother earth.
Abandonded haunted house
She lives in.
I be birth.
An *esp*.
I Believe, cold chilled
Demon.
Voodoo.
I Believe in the power.
Beyond the grave, they practise
Voodoo.
I am.
Windows fastened shut with big Nails
Plantation.

44.

I am
Unlikeable.
Eyes of stars,
Ethiopia.
I kissed him.
Long lost.
A pegasus outside of my window
Rainbow
Unicorn.
I am willing to destroy the Narnia witch.
Aslan, friend.
I kill her, the Narnia witch with Spells,
And prayers.
Locket.
Dark room With dark portraits
Of relatives.
I.   Unable to Contact my dead.

45.

Ive got spirits.
Spirits have I.
I see them.
Every night,
In this dark haunted house,
I am a witch.
Thou shall not syftet a wytch to live.
Yes.
Spirit.
Unholy
Blood on forehead.
A Touch of the wild.
I.

46.

Q
Who is the q?
Its a blackhaired
Ghostgirl.
Its a night Without
The Moon,
The q shines.
 Being.
A mathematical love.
I.   Birth.

47.

I a ghoul.
I a vampire
I a questionmark.
I a birth of universe
Clock in space,
Going backwards.
Let me Sail the sea
Of Rainbow, with my
Love.

48.

I an uncaring flower
Yours.
Dark castle.
I a burden.
I a faery
I a goblin
From the Forest,
And a girl Is going to the Woods.
To the Castle.
She is held back by creatures,
Goblins, faery and the dark beings
In the Woods. She is almost fallen.
Kissed the dark death huntress.
Moon.

49.

We are.
The like.
If the sea
Wherein the dying girl goes.
To lie on the beach, feel the sand
On her, the sunny side
Up.
She smiles, Her eyes full with stars
She borrowed from the witch.
Everything.
The is the evenstar.
The girl watches the stars.
She is flying as a faery.
Towards them.
Now soon the girl be a ghost.
Death came so swiftly to her.
A dark goblin write in the book of
Magick.
As he casts a spell, she gets to live.

50.

I am unable to die.
In the unbirthday, she is.
I artwork.
Wherein ghosts live.
And elves and goblins,
Faery.
Ghosts. Vittra.
Dark woods
Dark creatures.
I am.
A werewolf.